STARSPEAK

Messages of
ascension, love, contact and
more
in the words of our
star brothers and sisters

Dawn Henderson

This little book is dedicated to the beings of light from across the universe, our brothers and sisters from the stars, who are reaching out to us in this time of change, touching and guiding us with their love and wisdom.

We thank you

CONTENTS

AN INTRODUCTION...

There I was, happily working on my latest novel, when the star beings gave me a nudge. 'Put our messages into a book and get it out there.' But... I had other things to do. People were impatient for the book I was in the middle of writing. But the nudge came again, stronger this time. There was no point in arguing, they really wanted me to do this, so I gave in. I stopped what I was doing and got on with their book. And here it is...

My name is Dawn Henderson, and less than 18 months ago the crystal skulls and star beings of light exploded into my life. At first they were giving me information for my novel, Lost Legacy, but as time went on the messages became broader reaching, sharing information and guidance that they really wanted people on Earth to hear in this time of transformation. Who are the star beings of light? They are our galactic brothers and sisters – extra-terrestrials if you like – who are watching over and helping us.

Some of these messages – the majority in fact – are direct channellings, either received as I wrote, or as verbal channellings which were recorded and then transcribed. A few are passages taken from records of journeys I was taken on during meditations and information that was given to me there. Some were for personal guidance (and yes, those are staying private!), others – those I have included here – were intended to be shared with anyone who wished to hear them. And some were both.

In much of this work I was led and supported by a dear friend of mine, Sue Coulson (*www.crystalclearenergy.co.uk/*) and many of the italicised questions are hers. I have tried to put the information into categories but inevitably some blurring of boundaries has occurred. I have also given the names of the star beings who were speaking with me where I can. Some are my personal guides, others are occasional visitors who pop in when they have something they want to say. And as I'm typing this, my own guides are once more nudging me. They want me to introduce them.

The crystal skulls were my portal to the stars and they remain my primary tool for connecting with my star friends. With good reason: the crystal skulls and the star beings are very closely linked. (You can read more about this in Lost Legacy – *www.theskullchronicles.com*) Because of this, two of my star beings guides speak through crystal skulls of whom I am the caretaker.

Sirius Ra: connects with me through a black obsidian skull of the same name. He is a powerful being, Commander of the Sirian galactic fleet and member of the Galactic High Command. He is one of my close, long term guides and acts as gatekeeper to ensure that any being who wishes to speak through me is in alignment with my energy and is genuinely a being of love and light.

Akhtar: a star being from the great galaxy of Andromeda who also connects to me through another large, black obsidian skull. Akhtar is an immensely powerful being and an advisor to the Star Council of Light.

Kaluka: a personal guide, also from Andromeda, who helps me on my own journey as well as sharing messages for the people of Earth. He is not linked to any of the skulls, though often communicates with me through Sirius Ra.

.

ASCENSION...

AKHTAR (ANDROMEDA):
(The following is the transcript of a conversation with Akhtar, recorded live during the Sept 2012 Contact Convention in Avebury, England. I have left it in its entirety.)

Greetings my friends. It is good to see you all gathered here today. I am Akhtar, advisor to the Star Council of Light.

You know the time is nearly upon you, when you, and your world, and all around you will take that huge next step forward. The next step in your journey. The next step in your process. It is nothing to fear. It is something to rejoice, for it will take you on a journey that will open you up to experiences the like of which you have never experienced before.

You will still feel the same, look the same. Your world will not change. It does not need to. It is your own attitudes and perceptions that will change as you see more clearly the consequences of your actions. As you see more clearly that which you cannot at the moment see, hear that which at the moment you cannot hear, and feel that which at the moment you cannot feel.

You will be amazed at the activity that continues around you unseen in your present life, although not always unfelt. And in these changes within your perceptions and your actions, so the physical world around you *will* change. You will seek justice and equality. You will seek love and trust and co-operation. And in doing so, the wounds that have been inflicted on your people and your planet for so many years, for so many centuries, will begin to heal.

Do not fear that there is no time, that you must hurry. That you have run out of time. The situation upon your world is grave, but it is not irreversible. And the step that is so close upon you will allow this to be reversed, little at a time to begin with, but as the momentum grows, so the changes will speed. Do not be afraid of the state of your planet. Seek to ameliorate the damage where you may, but all will be healed in due course.

We are watching over you, and we are pleased with the progress. We wish to speak with more of you. We wish to communicate with more of you, and this is slowly happening for you are beginning to open your hearts and your minds to our presence.

You speak, many of you, of ascension as if it were an event, an event that happens over a day, or a month, or a year. We would say to you now, ascension is *not* an event. Ascension is a natural process, an on-going process, an endless process. When we first brought the skulls amongst you, so many years ago, you were but babies. Your awareness and your consciousness were barely above those of an animal, such as roam your fields and woodlands. You had a consciousness, and they had a consciousness, but it was not the level of human consciousness that we wished you to attain.

And it was at that point that your ascension began, all those many thousands of years ago.

But ascension is something that has been happening since the beginning. It is something that will happen until the end, for all is in ascension. For ascension is evolution, and evolution is a constant. We are ascending, everything in the universe is ascending, in that it is changing, and growing, and evolving.

Sometimes this process happens in small, gradual, barely perceptible steps. Sometimes it happens in large leaps, and it is this large leap that you are now facing. But it is a leap that is certain, that cannot be stopped. There are those who would interfere, who would seek to upset this process, but be assured that we will not allow this to happen, for affecting your process would affect the process of everything else.

And now I would ask the one named Sue, as she has been asked, does she have anything of which she wishes us to speak?

Akhtar, thank you for your presence, and I ask the question: Can you tell us why our planet is so important on such a large scale in the galaxies and the universe?
You are unique. You are unique in your ability to have complete free will. This is something that should be cherished. It is something that others would wish to take from you. It is something that needs to be shared and learned. While others, such as ourselves, may have a certain amount of leeway, we do not have the complete free will that you do. We, in the galaxy of Andromeda, a vast galaxy, a galaxy many times larger than your own, while we are all individual races, we are linked by a common consciousness, and it is this common consciousness that limits our own free will. It is something we

are used to. It is something that we accept and that does not adversely affect our lives, but still we cherish and value the gift that you have.

When we set the crystal skulls amongst you, it was in the knowledge that you could choose, and that you would choose, whether or not to accept them or reject them. To use them for the purpose for which they were designed, or use them for the purpose that could destroy you.

It is true that on several occasions we have taken action, when we felt that the latter was likely. It is why we will not allow them to come back to you until you are in a place where your free will will allow you to choose only light. But we will not bring them to you and tell you that this is what you must choose. We have never brought them to you and told you that this is what you must choose.

Akhtar, can you explain to us please how we can be connected on such a deep level with all existence in the universe and still have free will?
I cannot. I do not understand. For while we know much – we know *much* – we do not know all. There are some things that maybe it is better we do not know, for if we knew this then maybe we would seek it for ourselves, and this would disrupt the balance of our own societies and cultures.

Is there any last message that you would like to share with this gathering today?
We sense the openness of those gathered here. We sense the willingness of those gathered here. To hear our words, to connect with us, and to learn. We sense the openness of their hearts and the love that is amongst you. We say to you all now – we are here. We are amongst you. We wish to be with you, to learn from you as well as to teach you, for the ways of your

world are interesting, and new to many of us. And a puzzle in many ways too. Speak with us, send the intent to communicate with us, and we will gladly respond.

We hold you in our love.

$$\frac{}{} \quad \frac{}{} \quad \frac{}{}$$

KALUKA (ANDROMEDA):

(I recently attended a 'preparing for ascension' conference in Sedona, Arizona. This is one of the messages I channelled during the course of that conference)

Dearest ones,

We wish to speak of our joy and gratitude for your attendance at this conference, and for those who have created it through their will. Their will, their desire if you like, to share our words and our presence. To spread our messages of love and joy into the world. Their will and desire to share the joyous news of ascension and our brother/sister hood.

It is no coincidence that this event is happening at this time, for much love and light is needed to create the shift in energies on a global scale that is necessary to facilitate an easy shift into the higher dimensions. For though it will happen in any case – the frequencies are already at a level where this is no longer in doubt – the higher you can raise them before the final step in this part of the process, the less bumpy the ride will be.

Those of you who have been working with this, clearing, awakening, for some time, you will barely notice a thing. The frequency rise we speak of is to help those whose energies are not at such high levels. For them the ride may be more turbulent, as their readjustment will be more severe. It is for them then that raising the overall frequency of your world will be most advantageous.

We have heard many say that humans have free will and choice whether they will ascend or not. We say to you now, categorically and clearly: ALL WILL ASCEND. All who are on your planet at the moment of transition will ascend with Her. There is no choice in this. The choice was made long ago, before you incarnated into the human body you now inhabit. If you live and breathe at the moment of this step in the ascension process, YOU WILL ASCEND.

And we repeat this to you now so that there can be no misunderstanding – ALL WILL ASCEND. Your trees, your plants, your animals and other creatures, your oceans and rocks, your dear planet Herself, and all who live upon and within Her. You will ascend, and none will be left behind.

Others we have heard speak differently but this now we speak to you in truth. None will be left behind. None will be excluded. None will be 'transferred'. All are divine. All have chosen to be here at this moment. All have chosen to ascend. It cannot be otherwise for ascension is not exclusive; it is inclusive, fully and completely. Know this and rejoice in it.

We hold you in the arms of our love

꙳ ꙳ ꙳

ARGU:
Dear friends,

The future is much as the past, yet different in so many ways. Different in the way you think, in the way you perceive, in the way you act, and in the way you relate. The future is a future of the heart holding dominion over the head, of love vanquishing fear and all that fear brings with it, of inner knowing and personal power taking over from the edicts and laws of others outside of yourselves.

This will be the future, and yet it has already begun and will proceed at a rapid pace from here on. Those like yourselves who are willing to listen, to let go, and to learn, to see through new eyes and a new mind, through an open heart and clear sight, are already embracing this new way. Let your actions, your living, show others the way. Be a beacon that draws to it those who wish to know more, to learn of that which you embody.

There are many, many of you scattered across the surface of your world, shining your light like a candle; a candle whose flame grows ever stronger, does not diminish. Whose flame is a magnet and an inspiration.

Let the changes happen in their own time, for happen they will. They cannot be hastened, for people will only seek the light when they weary of the dark. Shine steadily, constantly, and allow others to draw to you, not seek to pull them through your will. Know that all is happening exactly as it was designed. Be still, and be at peace.

※　※　※

AKHTAR:

Greetings my friends,

You wish to know more of the ascension process. You wish to know how it is affecting your world and the people who live upon it.

Know that the process has been in motion since your world came into existence. It is on-going, with no beginning and no end. It is an evolution, a growth, a raising of frequencies. You are feeling some of the changes. The Earth herself, Mother Gaia, is preparing Herself for another great step forward. She is bringing Herself back into balance in many ways – energetically, in Her consciousness, and physically. This is the reason why there is so much that is perhaps unusual going on in the physical world. You have had many earthquakes. You have had some unusual volcanic activity. You have had much unusual climate activity. This is not to be feared, but to be accepted, for it is merely the Earth bringing Herself back into balance, and it will be short-lived. When balance is regained, such unusual activity will lessen, although you are aware that such activities, in some form, are the way of the world. It has always been, and it will always be so.

You are feeling the changes within your bodies, within your energy, those of you who are awake enough to feel and understand. But this is happening to everyone. To every animal, to every plant, to every human. It's just that you are more aware of it and of its causes than most. Allow it to be, dear ones, for it is necessary, and while at times it may be uncomfortable, it is not dangerous. It is merely you, and your energy, coming into balance, preparing for this big step that is ahead of you. For the ascension process is not a series of regular steps. It is a lot of small ones, followed by a big shift, followed by a lot of small ones, followed by another big shift, followed by a lot of small ones, followed by another big shift. And so on and so on, into infinity. You have been progressing through the little steps. Now you must prepare yourself for the big shift.

It will be uncomfortable perhaps for some, but it will not be dangerous or threatening. You will survive and you will all, your planet and everything upon it, the planets around you in your solar system, you will all make that shift together. And in actually making that shift you will not even remember it, you will not notice it. It is the step leading up to the shift that you will notice. Imagine it as an elastic band, and as you stretch further and further towards its extreme, it becomes tighter, and harder. But once that extreme is reached, and it is released, then everything flows forward easily and swiftly with no obstruction, and that is how it will be.

We on the Galactic Council of Light are watching over this process. We are easing it when we can, although we will not interfere in any major way, for this is a natural process and it does not need our interference. We are here to comfort and reassure those of you who are willing to connect with us. To watch out for the interference of sources that may not have the Earth's best interest at heart, for though this has not happened, it is always a possibility, and that is one of the reasons why we are here.

And we are also here to make contact with as many of you as we can, for in your next dimension, after this ascension shift, we will become much more visible to all of you. For your own frequency will rise and you will see things that you do not see now, hear things that you do not hear now, feel things that you do not feel now. And the more of you that are prepared, the easier it will be when that happens. And we are here because we are always wanting to protect and watch over you, to guide and to help you.

Many of you wish to see our presence on your world in physical form. Some do not believe this will happen; others are convinced that it will. We wish to say to you now that it will happen. It will happen very clearly and in ways where there can be no doubt. For we will come in many, many numbers so that none can pretend it hasn't happened and none can pretend that it is a ploy on behalf of someone else. But we will not come until you are ready. We will not come until enough of you have opened to our presence and accepted our existence that we will not cause turmoil, we will not cause excess violence, we will not cause aggression and threat to your planet. We say we will come soon, and we will, but we may not come, in fact it is unlikely that we will come, until you have made this shift to the next dimension. That will happen soon too.

But we will not say exactly when, for we know how much you humans enjoy deadlines and raise your expectations, and this cannot be. We will come when the time is right and when you are ready. Know this and let that be enough for now. We are pleased to be able to speak with you and to work with you. We are delighted that you are willing to work with us and that you wish to connect with us, and we give you our gratitude for this. We speak to you in love, always. Peace be with you all.

$$\rightarrow\!\!\!\ast \quad \rightarrow\!\!\!\ast \quad \rightarrow\!\!\!\ast$$

ASHAR (PLEIADES):

We come in peace and in love, seeking only to help and to guide you for you need our guidance and help now more than you have ever done. Your world is in turmoil, both in its body, the Earth, and in the structures and power systems you have created on it.

So it must be, for this is a time of great transformation and all change creates chaos and turmoil as the old makes way for the new. Sometimes, that which is cedes willingly to that which will be, and the transition is relatively calm. But in the face of such massive evolution as your planet is experiencing, the structures and edifices in place will try to hold on to what they have. They will not go without a fight.

But go they will as new winds sweep across the earth, cleansing and renewing the energies, awakening consciousness and reigniting the forgotten knowledge of humankind. In the face of such a tidal wave of higher vibrations, that which has had its day cannot survive. It too must evolve, grow and transform... or fall.

This is not a threat, or punishment, or warning, merely a statement of what is and what will be. Those who have woken to this change need not fear it and they will not, as they will see the perfect orchestration of its progress.

Those who are not yet awake need not fear either and yet they will, as they will not understand the beauty of this process. All they will see is the collapse of what they know, not the advent of a new and more benevolent way of being. They will fear the change and they will fear what may result.

We ask you who are awakening to share your knowledge and your love. Shine it into the world, for the more who understand, the easier and gentler this transition will be. Instead of fighting it, you will accept and even welcome it. Instead of holding on tightly, desperately, to what is, you will allow it to slip away. You will recognise the new energies coming in and use your knowledge and your wisdom to create a different, more harmonious and balanced way of being and seeing. You will finally begin to understand your true essence and reason for being. And you will understand the One-ness of all.

This time is upon us, the time for change. There is no room for error or delay. The process is in motion and all is changing. You too must change with it or fall.

How do we change?

Open your eyes to that which you do not see. Open your ears to that which you do not hear. Open your minds to that which you do not yet believe.

Over the next few months more massive upheaval will occur throughout your planet. Both in the Earth Herself and in the structures and power centres upon Her. This must be. It may be uncomfortable and frightening. It will certainly cause some degree of devastation but we ask that you understand its purpose and do not resist it.

The Earth is realigning Herself to new frequencies. And as She does so, so must all that live upon Her. So must the energetic structures on which your societies are based for they are founded on the old paradigm: a paradigm of fear, control and misused power. The new frequencies do not permit such outdated models to remain. They are of a lower and less evolved vibration.

We leave you now with the reassurance that, despite the turmoil, the future of your world and your kind is assured. You will learn the lessons and you will evolve into your new future. We speak in love.

$$\cdot\!\!\downarrow\!\!\cdot \quad \cdot\!\!\downarrow\!\!\cdot \quad \cdot\!\!\downarrow\!\!\cdot$$

KERULA:

The transformation you speak of, is it an on-going process, or is it a rapid change?

It is a finite process, but it is a lengthy process. It will have an end but it is not an overnight change.

What information can you tell us about the changes that are predicted to happen in this year, in our Earth time?

15

These changes are simply part of the on-going process. They cannot be stopped and it is not necessary to stop them, but it will not stop either at the end of the year. This is a process that will continue.

Can you tell us what changes we can expect to happen in this year?
Those who are already questioning, already awakening, already choosing to see, will find that the process evolves much more rapidly than it has before. There will be changes in the structure of many of the world's systems. They will not change completely but the changes will begin, as they have already, and they will continue at a pace that is gradual and acceptable and sustainable. Those who are not awakened, or who refuse to see, will find that they become more fearful of everything that is happening around them, but this must be.

Will this not cause a big split between those who are awake and those who are in fear?
No, for those who are awake will view those who are not with love and compassion. They will stay in their power and in their truth, and in doing so will help to awaken those who reside in fear and darkness. Again, a gradual process. There may be a split in opinions, but there will not be a split in reality. As more and more choose to stand on the side of light and awakening, so the see-saw, the balance, will slowly change in their favour. This is why we say there is no need to fear and that we believe the time is right for this transformation to occur.

UNNAMED STAR BEING:
Understanding energy, in all its forms, is of paramount

importance in the time that is to come. For understanding energy will be all. It will be how you live your lives. It will be the fundamental basis of all.

THE HIGH COMMAND OF THE GALACTIC COUNCIL:

Death does not have to be a violent passing. It can be a gentle letting go. It is your choice whether to fight the new, to fight what is coming in, to fight what cannot be avoided or to allow it to flow gently into your life and simply wash away what was there before. If you choose to battle, it will be difficult and it will be hard. If you choose to allow, it will be gentle and it will be easy. Each of you will experience it in your own way, according to your own choice.

Who is speaking now?
We are speaking

And what may we call you?
We are the High Command of the Galactic Council. Understand that we do not orchestrate this. We do not create this. We simply guide you in this, for it is happening beyond anyone's control. It is something that is in the natural order of things.

You speak of the change?
We speak of the change. We speak of the change that is coming in now to your world and has been coming in for some time. We speak of the change that is increasing in momentum and in intensity. We speak of the change that cannot be avoided and that must happen.

And do you foresee where this change will lead us?
This change will lead you forward on the path that you were always going to follow, the natural evolution of things.

Can you speak to us any words that would tell us what to expect along this path?
What you expect will be what you expect. In other words, what you think it will be is how it will be. Your opinion, your beliefs will create the outcome.

The time of the old ways is over. They must fall to allow new, sustainable ways of being. To allow a new way of relating and to being in your world. They must fall and they will fall and these changes will come about. How they will come about and how they will fall all very much depends on how you choose to see them and what you create. If you choose to look at these changes with fear, then times will be difficult, they will be troubled and they will be uncomfortable for you. If you choose to allow them and to accept them without fighting, seeing that they are for the best and that any turbulence is merely temporary, then it need not be that way. The changes will just gradually happen and happen easily.

Are these changes within our physical bodies as well as within our physical world?
These changes are within your energy. Changes within these vibrations of energy will yes create changes in your physical body, but changes for the better.

When can we expect these changes to be noticed by the masses on this planet?
Many of the masses will not notice. They will be in such fear that all they will see is the difficulties and the upheaval. They will not see the positive changes that are coming out of them. The changes within yourselves will be gradual and it will not

be until looking back from a distance that you understand how they have affected you.

Is there anything we can do to ease this process on a personal level?
Accept. Allow. Keep your vibrations at the higher end of the spectrum as much as you can for that is where you are moving to. If you can create those vibrations for the majority of the time in your body, it will be a natural and easy transition for you.

These higher vibration states, do they mean we can live our lives in a different way to what we do now?
It means you will be focussed on the elements of love and joy and one-ness. It means you will be able to let go more easily of the fear and everything it brings with it. It means that illness and disease will be less prevalent for at a higher vibration they will find it harder to take root in your body. These things are caused to a very great extent by fear and all it brings. You step out of fear and into love and those illnesses will not be part of your life. Do the things you love. Do the things that lift your heart, lift your spirit and make your soul sing. View the world with love. Treat everything that happens to you as a gift, even when it is uncomfortable for you, for the gift is always there. If you look for the gift and not at the negative then you will see it and you will not fall back into a lower vibration.

Is there anything else that you can share with us about this today?
We wish to say that these changes have been happening for many years now and many of you who are doing this work are aware of this. These changes will come about for many years to come, for it is a slow and gradual process. We ask you to stay firm in your trust of what you know in your heart. To not

allow yourselves to be swayed by the mass consciousness that does not understand. The more you stay in your heart and in your soul, the more you can change that consciousness for the better, for your energy will spread out into the world and touch it in many ways. It is important now that as many of you as possible stay in that space of love and trust and belief and truth, for it will ease the passage of these changes.

* * *

PLEIADIAN:

The world you live in draws a distinction between what you see and what you imagine. You believe what you see. You do not believe what you imagine. You feel that what you see is true and what you imagine is untrue. And this is the lesson that you must unlearn. You feel you cannot believe until you see but you cannot see until you believe.

* * *

UNNAMED STAR BEING:

We wish you to speak, to tell the world of the skulls and of the light beings from the stars. Of what is happening on your planet and why and what it means for humanity.

Can you share with us some words about that now? What will it mean for humankind?

It will mean a future unlike anything you can imagine, unlike anything you have ever imagined. It will be unlike anything you have ever experienced. It will be harmony. It will be peace. It will be justice and equality. It will be co-operation and compassion, much of which is lacking on your planet at the moment. And this is OK. It is part of your evolution.

And I'm seeing forests. In the forests are, almost like towers, circular buildings on towers, on stilts. And people are living amongst the tree tops in these places. And they're living very much in harmony with the world around them. There are so many trees. The lands are covered with trees.

Do the trees hold significance?
The trees are the life force of the planet. The trees are the secret to Gaia's survival. They are Her heartbeat and Her breath. The trees will return as they once were. Trees will once more cover the Earth.

Do you have a sense of knowing how long this will take?
I see 200 years, maybe a little more, but it will be in time.

And does the human species still exist here at that time?
Yes. We thrive, but we are many fewer in number. Through choice. We choose to keep our population levels to a level that is sustainable. We choose to limit the number of children that we bring into the world, to maintain this balance. And it will be easy to do so. It will be a choice that none will think about because it will be so obvious and so unthinkable.

✢ ✢ ✢

LOVE...

9th DIMENSION PLEIADIAN ENERGY BEINGS:

What is it that you can help us learn?

Trust. Peace. Understanding. Understanding on a deep level. A soul level. A heart level rather than a conscious thought level. We can help you to do so, if you will allow us.

And what must we do to allow this to occur?

Simply be still and feel our presence. Feel us touching those hearts.

And why is this of benefit to us?

Because this is the time when your hearts must be opened. And it is easier to open a heart that is filled with peace than a heart that is filled with pain. You are moving from a thought-based existence to a heart-based existence.

And is it possible for you to tell us how close we are to opening our hearts fully?

Some of you are close, and some of you are far. We feel that those in the room today are close but you have not learned, you are not yet able, to keep it open constantly and consistently. This is what you must learn to do.

Can you help us with this?

This is something that you must practise. We will be here to support you. We will lend our energy to you, but this is something that you must be aware of and practise. You must learn to feel when your heart is closed, or when it is closing through fear. And you must make the decision, the choice, to allow it to open. To look away from that which is causing the pain and towards that which will bring the love that will allow this opening.

And can you give us something specific to focus on, to remind us to head towards love?

To remind you to head towards love, you must first recognise when you are not in love. You must practise being aware. We cannot give you anything to remind you to be aware. That must come from your own feelings, from your own choices and from your own intention. The more that you do it, the more that you practise, the more you will sense it and the easier it will become.

Allow your heart to expand. Allow the feeling in your heart to expand. Allow it to fill your body and to chase away that which is not love from every cell. For your heart has more power than you can imagine. The heart is the most powerful organ in your body and commands the most powerful force in the universe.

Can you help us to understand a process to help us to stay more connected with our heart energy, one we can share with others?

You must feel love, anchor that feeling in your body so that you can access it at any time. Remember how it feels to allow pure love to flow through you. And you all have a sense of how that feels, whether you remember it consciously or whether it is hidden in your sub-conscious. You have all experienced at some point that pure, powerful love. Access it, anchor it, and remember it. And draw on it when you seek to open your heart further.

And in our everyday existence, is it possible for us to walk around with a fully expanded heart?
Yes. And you need not fear that it will put you in danger or make you vulnerable, for a fully expanded heart is the greatest and most powerful form of protection that you can possibly possess. For where the love flows openly and freely, then no negative matters will touch you.

When you walk with an open heart, you affect all those around you, and whether they feel it or not, their hearts will begin to open more. It cannot be otherwise. Your open heart is the catalyst for the opening of the hearts of all those you meet, even if just in a very small way.

And is there anything else you can tell us about this energy today?
It is the power of creation. It is the energy that created the universe as you know it, and yet it is not that which you recognise as love in your daily lives. For the love that you speak of in general, the love that your humankind speaks of, is only a tiny fraction of what is available to you. And you have put so many conditions and definitions and limitations and negative emotions attached to love. This is a distorted version of the reality.

The love that we speak of is more than you could ever conceive, but you can touch a part of it and you can allow it to flow through you whether you understand it or not.

When you connect with who you are in your deepest being, you connect with love, but you cannot process everything it brings up in you for it would just cause you to go into overload. So you feel just a small part of it, and often that, in itself, is overwhelming enough.

ASHAR (PLEIADES):

Why is there so much talk about heart-centred awareness at this time?

Because it is a vital process in your evolution and your awakening. The heart is the centre of all. Love is the creative force of the Universe. Without it you cannot move forward. You are being asked to let go of your fear. When you let go of something, you must replace it with something else. When you let go of fear, what must come into its place is love, for that is its opposite. Love is what holds the world together. It is what creates the universe. It is the force that created initially. It is the fabric of all. It is the essence of all.

Can you explain that to us more? How can a feeling be the fabric and the essence of all?

Love is not a feeling. Love is an energy. Love is THE energy. When you feel love, you feel a feeling, but it is so much more than that which you feel within your bodies. You sense and you feel a part of what love can be and of what love can do. That is how you feel it in your bodies.

And how is it portrayed into other dimensions if it's different?

It is that which holds everything together, for love is a magnet. Fear pushes apart, love pulls together, and it is so in whatever dimension that you exist.

You speak of it as a creative force. Is it part of the energy that we use for deliberate creation?

It is, for when you desire with joy, joy and love are closely linked. There is only love and fear, so when you are looking forward to something in a positive energy, you must be summoning love. It cannot be any way else. When you are creating from a negative place, you must be summoning fear. That cannot be any way else either.

And how can we help to teach others about love?
You must live your words and your beliefs. You must live your truth. You must show by example but you must also teach people to open their hearts. For when their heart chakras are truly open, their heart energy centres, that is when divine love, universal love, unconditional love, will flow. That is when they can experience what love truly is.

Is there a process, a method or tool that we can use to help activate out hearts fully?
There are many tools and you use some of them. Crystals, sound, nature. Being in nature opens your heart.

Can I ask why?
Because the energy of nature is one of creation. And love is the energy of creation, therefore they are one and the same.

Is it significant that our plants and our trees are green?
The energy of the heart is green. You are correct.

Do other colours have different influences on the heart energy?
The heart energy is green. Other colours may come and go but it will always remain in that state of balance and love.

And can I ask about the colour pink? How does that interact with the human energy?
It soothes. Pink is the colour of compassion. Compassion is a very powerful element.

Is compassion and love the same thing?
In your world it is very closely linked, but love is so much more than that. It is closely linked to what you consider love, but you do not understand the true nature of love. Love is everything. Compassion is only a small part of that.

Can you speak some words to us now that will help us to understand more fully the nature of love?
Love is all there is. Love is creation. Love is one-ness. Love is the essence of all and of who you are. Without love, there would be nothing, for nothing could exist as it is the fabric of the universe. Without it there would be no fabric and no universe.

I know you wish me to explain further but there is nothing more to say. That is all that there is.

I hear your words but my brain is struggling to comprehend.
You cannot comprehend with your brain. You can only comprehend with your heart.

CONTACT...

KALUKA:

We speak with you to prepare you for the physical coming of the star beings, which will not be long. To pave the way both by communicating with you both on a telepathic level and showing you physical evidence that we are soon to arrive among you.

We understand that many of you who are receiving our words at this time are fearful of speaking out loud, are fearful of speaking publicly. You have fear of ridicule, of scorn, of rejection. We are here to help all of you who are undertaking this task to gain the confidence and belief you need, the strength you need, to do this.

For we wish you to speak of our presence amongst you, both in our physical and non-physical form. That is the most important task that you can do at this moment, for when we come, us and our brothers and sisters amongst the stars, the more of you who are aware of our presence and kindly nature, and our wish to do no harm and to impose no will upon you, the more you will quell the panic of those who do not yet understand.

Hold us with love in your hearts. Hold our messages and mission with love in your hearts. For in this way you will share your belief and your understanding with others in a way that they are able to understand.

We will help all who ask for our help. If you are lacking in confidence or belief, or you have a fear of standing up and speaking out, then call on us, for we will listen and we will be here with you. We are always here but only when you speak with us can we help. We will not help, we will not interfere, unless you ask us. That is not our way. You have the free will to choose or not to choose.

But we do ask you to speak. To speak of us. It may be that you speak of us publicly. If you cannot do so, then speak of us privately. Speak of us to just a few of those who you know may be willing to understand and to listen. For as they hear, and they become convinced in their turn, so they will speak. And thus forth, and thus forth, like a pebble rippling out its waves in the pond.

Can you speak more about the showing of the star beings upon the Earth, what some call disclosure? Through many channels, many star beings are speaking of their wish to be open upon the Earth

When we will come openly to you, there will be no mistaking it. We will come in great numbers. Many will feel threatened by those numbers, for it is beyond their comprehension that this could possibly be. But we do not come in aggression. We do not come to overthrow or to dominate. We come merely to show of our presence. That there are many, many beings in this universe other than yourselves. We come to you with open hearts that we may help you, and to show that we are willing to help you. Willing to help the humans and your world at this time. In this time of transition, in this time of change, in this time of turmoil, we are here to help. And when we come, you will see.

Can you speak a little of the reaction you expect from those upon the Earth, when this event takes place?
We hope to be received in joy and friendship, but we know that that is a wish that will not be fulfilled, for there is much fear on your Earth. There is much disinformation spread through your films and your news about the intent of those who would come to your planet from afar.

We will be met with anger. We will be met with fear. We will be met with more than fear, with terror, by many, for they will fear the worst of us. That is why you, and those like you, who know the truth of our being, who know the truth of our presence and our coming, must hold strong. For it is true, dear one, that even you and those like you may well feel fear when faced with the reality of our physical presence, for it is so unlike When we will come openly to you, there will be no mistaking it. We will come in great numbers. Many will feel threatened by those anything you have ever experienced before. And though, while you know it will be, the reality of it is very different from the knowing of it.

Stand firm in your truth. Stand firm in your knowing. Stand firm in your love. And while you may feel the fear, know that the fear is an untruth and that the reality lies behind it.

Allow yourself to step through the fear. Allow yourself to access the love that we bear, to step into your true being as a star soul, and to greet us as brothers and sisters.

We hold you in much love.

ASHTAR (HIGH COMMAND OF THE GALACTIC COUNCIL):

At the conference I attended this week, many people, so many people, are desperate to see their star brothers and sisters walk amongst us. And it is something I would wish, though maybe I do not have that desperation, but it is something that I would wish to see. Can you tell me, will this happen, and will this happen soon?

Oh dearest ones, you do not truly understand. You do not truly understand perfect timing, necessity of timing, the need for patience. We have told you many times that we will come and walk amongst you, and this is a promise that we make to you, that we will do so. But we will NOT do so until the time is right. And we cannot tell you when that time will be, for it will depend solely on the people of the Earth and their readiness to welcome us without fear.

At this time, though the light is spreading, there would be too many who are too fearful to accept our presence. The majority would be too fearful to accept our presence. It would cause violence, it would cause fear, it would cause more darkness to spread and we will not cause darkness. We are of the light, and we will NOT cause darkness. Even among the enlightened ones amongst you, those who are more conscious and have been working on themselves for many, many years to bring themselves to the higher vibration that is needed for them to be able to guide others through the process of ascension, there is fear. Perhaps not fear of us, but fear of the darkness, fear of those who work against us, fear of what may happen in this ascension process. You have noticed this yourself. You have commented on it to us yourself. Within so many of the beings of love and light, even such as those with you on the conference, there sits a pool of fear. You sensed it, and you were correct. It exists. Not among them all, but among some. We would even say, among many. There is fear of what will happen, there is fear about what they must give up, what they must leave behind. There is fear.

Their fears are foundless for you do not have to give anything up. You do not have to leave anything behind. But while the fear exists there is a risk that they will create that, create that very reality within their own life. We would not wish this.

We will not show ourselves until we are sure one hundred per cent, totally, completely sure, that your world is ready to receive us with open arms and in the spirit with which we come to you. But we will say this, and we will make this promise to you. There are those amongst you who are open, who are willing and who are without fear at the process that lies ahead. There are those amongst you who are without fear at seeing us walk amongst you and in time, and perhaps not too much time, we will show ourselves to individuals. Not so that our appearance and presence may be broadcast, for that would serve no purpose to see us extra-terrestrials moving amongst you. To speak of it on a grand scale, on a worldwide scale, would serve no purpose. But we will come, we will visit, with many of you who are truly open to our presence.

And by truly open I do not mean that you will not have some little anxiety and fear when something unusual appears amongst you, for in many ways that is natural. When I say open, I speak of those whom despite the fear and the anxiety it may create, will know the truth of us in the depths of their hearts and their souls, and will turn to us with open arms, welcome us with open arms and open hearts, seeing us as your true galactic family, your brothers and sisters from the stars, and accepting us totally and completely. We cannot say who these people are. We will not say who these people are, but they will be the ones who we can trust not to cause drama, not to wish their stories for personal glory, recognition, their five minutes of fame. We will come to them, we will speak with them, heart to heart, soul to soul. We will answer questions, we will show ourselves, but we will not stay. We will leave no trace of our visit so that there will be no proof, except in the hearts and minds of those we visit, that we have ever been here. At least until the time is right when we appear to you all.

WORDS OF
ENCOURAGEMENT...

SIRIUS RA (SIRIUS):

Dearest ones,

Do not worry, for in worry you give strength to that which you worry about. Free your mind. Allow it to fly free from the shackles of fear and disquiet. Allow it the clarity and freedom to receive the guidance you are asking for, guidance that cannot be heard while your mind is filled with heavy thoughts.

Be open and free to follow where the winds of intuition carry you, without agenda or preconception. Trust in yourself, in that knowing that lies rooted deeply and always within you. Do not act without consideration, but let that consideration stem from the wisdom of your heart, and not from the complex, linear computations of your mind. For your mind can only act on what it already knows and thus stands within its limitations. The heart has no such limitations, acting instead on dreams, on love and on the eternal wisdom of all, and not the pre-programmed possibilities of the intellect.

SIRIUS RA:

Allow your world to expand. Do not fear the consequences in doing so, for in staying small, in staying shut away in your safe little boxes, you serve no-one. Least of all yourselves.

Now is the time when all who are awakening, when all who hear the call of their heart and their soul to become more than they now are. To step out of the shadows and into the light. To take the steps on the path they long ago chose to take. Now is the time to set your fears aside and to take those steps.

The world needs you, as it has always needed those who refuse to conform, who dare to think beyond the confines of that which is considered safe, or possible, or even right. And now, in this time of such change, of such powerful transformation of the energies that are the foundation of all existence, now it is even more necessary.

To those of you who see your road but have not yet found the courage to walk it, we say to you – take those steps. They are not as difficult as they seem from the place where you now stand. Take those first steps and see how easy and joyful it can be.

And to those of you who hold a powerful desire to step forward, to break free of the shackles that hold you to a way of being that no longer serves you, we say – ask us for our help, and we will guide you. Listen to the stirrings of your heart and soul, for they are our voices guiding you. Take just one small step towards that which draws you and allow the path then to illuminate itself in front of you, one step at a time.

You do not need to know your final destination, although we understand it is a human desire to do so. Allow the uncertainty to be present, immerse yourselves in the adventure of your journey, and allow the joy these first steps bring to fill you. Soon you will see, but for now, just step forward.

We hold you in our love

SIRIUS RA:

Be at peace. For when you are at peace – when peace holds dominion within your own heart and your own being – then it emanates from you and touches the world around you.

You do not need to do anything other than be at peace. And it need not be difficult, for peace is the essence of you, the companion of love. It lies within you simply waiting to be touched, and when you touch it, it illuminates your being so that you become a beacon to all those who seek it and have not yet found it. Who have not yet discovered that it lies within them too and that all they need to do to find it is to be still and allow it to emerge.

Your peace will aid this emergence, little by little, in all who come into contact with you. And this is how peace will spread in your world.

SIRIUS RA:

Prepare yourselves. Prepare yourselves for the changes that are coming. The changes that you know in your deepest heart to be real.

All is changing. Be grateful that it is so. For while nothing will be as it has been, the transformations you see unfold over the times to come will be joyful, and willingly embraced by those who are aware enough to understand.

Make time to raise your consciousness, your vibration. To open your hearts and minds.

You are already doing this – we ask you now to make it your priority, your focus, and to do it more. Ask us to help you, to guide you and to strengthen you. For we are always with you.

※ ※ ※

SIRIUS RA:

Dearest friends,

There is really nothing for me to say that you do not already know. No guidance that you have not yet received.

So I simply repeat to you – open your hearts and receive. Receive all the blessings of the Universe in all their diverse forms and in all their glory. These will be yours without limit when you allow your hearts to fully open and your minds to expand.

See love, feel love, everywhere, even in those situations you find uncomfortable or unpleasant. For it is there. Look. Look closely, in the knowing that it is there, however well concealed below appearances. Look, and you will find it.

Do not get caught up in appearances. Look beyond. Look deeper, for that is where the truth lies concealed. Look past the surface, look past your fears, look past accepted truths and beliefs to what is hidden beneath. Only then will you begin to see clearly. Only then will you begin to understand.

It is too easy to become caught up in appearances, in their illusion. To stop there and go no further. If you can understand that appearance is just the first layer, and not the whole, you will be able to perceive more deeply, to explore more deeply, to understand more deeply the truth that is there for all who wish to see.

SIRIUS RA:

Dear souls,

We, the star beings of light, do not ask that you set aside the wonders and pleasures of your physical world, or of your physicality, in order to work with us, as many of you feel you should. It is true that there are some amongst you who are prepared to dedicate their lives fully to the task before them, but they are few, and it is not necessary. Allow yourselves to live your physical lives, to embrace and delight in them. We would not wish it otherwise.

The work before you is important, vital even, but it need not be all-consuming. We ask only that you find a balance, that the physical does not overshadow the unseen, and vice versa. At times, one may dominate the other, but then it will change about, as it must.

The physical is needed for grounding, and the more, the higher, you work with us, the greater your need will be to return to the physical and to immerse yourself in it. A foot in both worlds, a step in both worlds, each complementing and enhancing the other. For as you move into higher dimensions and higher frequencies, your enjoyment of, and appreciation for, your physical world will grow. And as you ground yourselves ever more firmly in your physical world, so your connection to us will increase and strengthen, and the dimension heights you can attain will soar.

✳ ✳ ✳

THE HIGH COMMAND OF THE GALACTIC COUNCIL:

We simply wish you to know that when we set our project in motion for your world, so long ago, we wished only for peace and harmony, but we also knew that we would have to leave you to evolve in your own way. We have been watching over you. Watching your progress. You have made mistakes but you have also made wonderful progress. And mostly you have learned from the mistakes that you did make. You are now at a time when you need to look back on the mistakes of your past centuries. You understand where you have perhaps deviated from the path that we wished for you. It is our hope, it is our wish, that you can let go of the fear and the anger and the greed that is destroying your societies and to open yourself up to co-operation, love and harmony. It is our belief that you can achieve this and, although it seems like a huge task, it need not be, for your essence is love. And as you find it within yourself, so it spreads to those around you.

So we ask you now, you who are hearing us, who are feeling us, who are sensing this change, to work with us in this. Push back the boundaries of the darkness and the fear and allow the light to shine once more on your planet.

GUL (GRAND COUNCIL OF THE GALACTIC ALLIANCE):

We feel that your future, the future of the people of your world, is very positive and good. We see changes. We see changes continuing for many years and many lifetimes, and every change carries you in a forward way to a better life and better understandings. There is much work for you here, much for you to do and accomplish in these next months and years. Do not be afraid to undertake it for it will bring you great rewards and much joy. You have a task, you all have a task, those of you who are in this place and this work. An important task, but it will not be an onerous one. It will be a task that brings you love and joy and great delight. You are the spearhead of the new beginnings that is upon you. And it is a place of honour to be standing at the forefront of these changes. Know that you are more than worthy of the job. Know that you are more than able to undertake and succeed in all that you have been asked to do and that you have taken on.

KOORM, 7th DIMENSIONAL BEING:

Take our words and hold them in your heart. Leave them there and return to them often so that when fear comes upon you, you can turn to them and you can feel their truth and the fear will leave. There are many beings around you, beings who wish you to succeed, but also to thrive. They are there for you. Simply ask for their support when you are feeling fear. Simply ask for their love and to be able to feel their presence, and you will know that you have their support and their help.

HAMISH, A NON-GALACTIC GUIDE:

You must follow where you are guided, even if at times that feels like you are taking a detour that you do not wish to make or that you feel is taking you away from where you ought to be. For all is relevant and all is important. And these forays into seemingly unrelated areas will provide you with information that will be of help and that you will at some point see is closely connected to your path.

You sense that there is much waiting ahead of you, much excitement and adventure that you cannot see yet and yet you do not believe it. We say to you now, your lives are unfolding. Follow it and do not worry where it is taking you or what might be at the end. Enjoy the journey as you go and enjoy your destination when you reach it. This we speak for all of you who are here today.

We ask you to hold on to that sense of excitement and anticipation , for that will bring you the passion and enthusiasm to get on with the work that is in front of you. To commit yourself to it. And you must commit for it is important both for you personally and to the world.

ADRAEUS OF THE PETRIDES:

Dearest children of the universe,
Have faith. Faith in the future that awaits you – a future of understanding, enlightenment and co-operation. A future where the living beingness of your world is recognised and the interconnectedness of all is made sacred.

Believe in this future, in a time when light dominates and darkness, fear and suffering recede. When humankind acknowledges the presence of her star brothers and sisters and welcomes them to its world. For it is waiting, and it will be. You have taken enough steps for such a future to no longer be in doubt. It will not happen tomorrow, nor perhaps next year, but it will be. Have faith that it is so.

RA:

Dearest ones,

Your faith is requested. Your faith is necessary. Faith in us, faith in yourselves, and faith in the bonds that hold us together. In the love we hold for you and our desire that you flourish. And in your own power, which you do not yet truly see.

Your power is immense. Some of you see us as higher beings than you, superior even. This is not so. We are more conscious, yes, more aware of our power and of our divinity, but it is no greater than yours. We see and we know things that you as yet do not. This does not make us more than you. It is simply that we have learned these things and you as yet have not.

We ask you for your love and respect yes, but no more than you would of another of your own kind. We would ask you for your trust and that you allow us to guide you from our place of greater understanding. But do not mistake this place that we stand and one you yourselves cannot be. Do not consider us as holding wisdom and knowledge you yourselves cannot hold.

You are our brothers and sisters, equals in merit and divine being. Know that this is so.

ADRAEUS:

Hold firm to your dreams. Hold firm to your beliefs. Hold firm to your truth. Even when those around you call you crazy and try to bring you back into their reality, hold firm. For their truth, their reality, belongs to a world that is on the brink of transformation. It is a truth and a reality that will soon cease to exist, although it may remain in their perception for a while to come.

However out on a limb it feels that you are sitting at this moment, know that more are joining you there daily as they awake to a new truth and a new reality. The change is happening, it is well underway, and soon the primary transformation will be complete. From this all will follow – all must follow – and the new paradigm will come into being, will crystallise in the consciousness of all. Then, my friends, you new world will truly be a reality.

EARTH MATTERS...

OLAN (PLEIADES):

The Earth is a mother ship that will carry you forward on your journey. You must learn to work with Her and communicate with Her, to hear Her wisdom and Her guidance as well as that of the beings from other worlds. She will help you if you listen.

Is there a specific way to connect with her?

Be in contact with Her. Go to those points and places where Her energy is strong and unpolluted. Go in silence and in solitude, or at least in small groups where you can be silent and together, for crowds, while they are beneficial for raising Her energy and healing, do not help when it comes to connecting with Her and communicating with Her. There are many places on the land where you may touch Her, feel Her, but it is helpful often to go to those places where the energy is strongest. Those places that are known to be Her pulse. Then simply sit, speak, listen, feel and become as one. Do not rush. Do not become impatient for She will speak to you. She will speak to you with love, with tolerance and with patience. For She understands that the wrongs that have been committed on Her were made through ignorance and lack of understanding.

ASHAR:

Can the consciousness of humans affect the consciousness of Gaia?

Yes, when human consciousness is in agreement, when there is a mass cohesion of thought, but also there must be enough humans on the planet for it to override the consciousness of Gaia herself, which is powerful.

Many see Gaia's consciousness as damaged or broken at this time. Is this true?

No, Gaia's consciousness is whole. It is simply your perception. The planet is damaged, yes, but her consciousness is not. She welcomes your healing, but with or without it, she will come back into balance.

Would it be of benefit to humans for them to partake in healing of Gaia?

Yes, for if she brings herself back into balance, there may be no humans remaining on the planet. She will do what she must do to heal herself.

And have positive steps been taken in this direction recently, or is there still very much to do?

There is still much to do, but humankind is moving in the right direction. More and more of you are waking up to the understanding that she is a living, conscious being. Are waking up to the understanding that you have hurt and injured her and that she requires healing on all levels. This awareness will grow. It is growing rapidly already. There are many out there now, seeking to heal her through many different means, and this is a very positive step forward for her and for you.

Is there anything else you can tell us about this at this time?
It is important that you send love and healing in your thoughts for this is a powerful form of energy and intention. It is important that you understand that she is a being, conscious and aware, and that you share this understanding with those who are ready to hear. We do not ask that you all make it your mission, for we know that there are other things that you are here to do, though for many of you, this *will* be your task. Just simply allow it to be part of your conversations and your understanding, and allow this understanding to flow. We ask that you act in ways that are loving and kind to the world that you live on and seek to make your mark on her surface be as light and as gentle as possible. We understand that there are limits because of the way that your lives are run and your society is structured and your culture works, but we ask that you do what you can, for every little step is a big step forward.

KALUKA:

Dear friends,

The Earth is changing. Some ways you can see and measure – your climates, the temperature, desertification and the melting of the ice caps for instance. Others are invisible, sometimes happening below the surface, sometimes solely energetically. For the Earth too is preparing herself for ascension, and to do this she must rebalance and re-harmonise, taking into account the damage inflicted on her surface by mankind over many hundreds of years.

Be assured, this damage IS only skin deep, but it must be challenged and healed, cared for, in the same way that damage to your own surface, your skin, must be cared for in order to avoid deeper, more serious infection. So it is with the Earth.

You may find many of these changes difficult and uncomfortable at times. This is the price you must pay for your past and your continuing misuse of your world. They will be short-lived but will grow more intense before they once more ease. Be prepared, sit it out, and do what you can for your part to help in this healing, whether through direct action or by sending love and healing to wherever it is needed.

Follow your own heart and your own guidance as to what you must do, do not simply follow blindly where your leaders would have you go. For they are often misinformed and unknowing at best, following their own unhelpful agendas at worst. Trust in your own knowing, ask the Earth what She would have you do, and trust in that.

$$\downarrow\kern-0.3em\uparrow \quad \downarrow\kern-0.3em\uparrow \quad \downarrow\kern-0.3em\uparrow$$

KOORM:

Is it possible from your dimension to see beyond our physical time and space to what we would call our future?
To a certain extent, although that is not something we are habituated to do. What is it that you wish to know?

I just merely wish to know if the great changes that are happening with energy of the Earth will be reflected in its surface? Can we expect great change on a physical level?
There will be... We can see there will be changes and upheaval on the physical level. As the vibrations shift, you may experience changes in the surface of the planet in the way of earthquakes and other disruptions. But this will only be temporary. As time goes on, as humankind awakes and

becomes more aware of its environment, these things too will change. But this is a process and not a sudden change. You will become more aware of your environment and you will care for it more.

One question I'm hesitant to ask is hearsay from others who predict in our world big changes due to electro-magnetic changes within our Earth - pole shifts of the earth and the sun.
The pole shifts are natural phenomena that have happened on your planet many times in the past, but we do not foresee this happening in the immediate future. At some point it must occur, it has to. It is part of how your world behaves. But it is not something for you, or your children, or your children's children, to think about.

Can you give us any practical advice about how we can best spread the message of love to those outside of our current experience?
You speak a message most effectively through your actions rather than your words. Your words are important but begin to live your truth. Begin to live your life only in love. Others follow more by those who lead by example than from those who lead from words. And while your words will teach, your actions will inspire.

YOUR PHYSICAL
WORLD...

KALUKA:

Kaluka, how are the ascension processes affecting our physical bodies at this time?

In many ways, dearest one, for all is changing and as all changes, so must you change. Your physical structure is changing, the density of your cells is changing, the vibration of your cells is changing. This may create discomfort within you, within all of you, for you are all going through this process at this time. Not just some of you, not just chosen ones, not just those who are ready and conscious of it. Know that you are all going through the changes at this time, for this is something that your world is going through, and as your world is going through it, so is all upon it, whether that be plant or animal or human.

How are these changes affecting our physical bodies?

You may experience aches and pains as your body adjusts. You may find things that were once comfortable to be uncomfortable, and things that were once uncomfortable to become comfortable. You may find specific difficulties with certain things. We know that for some, your eyesight is being affected and we say to you that this is just a temporary thing. As your inner sight adjusts, so must your outer sight change, and it takes a while for the physical to catch up with the energetic, and this is in all things with regards to your body. The energetic changes happen first, which create the sensations, and then your physical body must change. But it can only change at a slower rate, for such is the nature of physical matter.

And which foodstuffs will most help us, and which foodstuffs are not helpful to us at this time in easing this process?
Your body will tell you that, for it will change from day to day and even hour to hour. The changes are not constant. They fluctuate. Everything is happening in a wave, in a form, in a ripple, and what is good and helpful for you today may not be so tomorrow.

Learn to listen to yourself. Learn to listen to what your body is asking you. And do not say 'no' just because it is something that you have previously thought, or been told, is unhealthy for you. If your body desires it, then your body requires it, and it would be helpful for you to listen and to follow that advice. We are hearing your thoughts about whether you should be eating the so-called 'unhealthy' foods you crave and whether this need is a result of this process and a consequence of these changes. We would say to you, sometimes it is so, and sometimes it is not so. This is another time that you must learn to listen to the truth of your body.

There are times when you will desire these things when your body will require these things. And there are times when you will desire these things and your body will not need them.

Learn to discriminate. Discern between the two and all will be well. Go with the flow. It is a phrase we have heard much among your humankind. It is one of your favourite sayings, many of you, and it is a wise one. Go with the flow, listen to the needs of your body, and heed them.

If you crave sunshine, then seek sunshine. If you crave sleep, then seek sleep. If you crave the green of the woodlands and countryside, then seek the green of the woodlands and countryside. And if you crave the grounding hit of a chocolate bar to bring you into the physical when you have spent too much time connecting with us and allowing your feet to float from the ground, or in your head, thinking, then allow yourself to have the sudden hit of a chocolate bar.

Does ascension mean moving into another dimension with our physical bodies?
It does mean entering another dimension with your physical body, but it does not mean disappearing from the Earth. For all will ascend, and all will ascend at the same time, whether they understand that they are doing so or not. It is not something that one will do and another will not. The world will ascend. The world *is* ascending, and as the world ascends, so everything upon its surface ascends with it. So, although you will move into different dimensions, into higher dimensions, so will all that around you. You will not disappear, and it will not disappear. It will accompany you, and that is how it should be.

Are you working to recalibrate us as we sleep?
We are, dearest one. And we are aware that many of you are experiencing sleep disorders, sleep disturbances. You do not always sleep well, waking at strange times for no reason. Waking early for no reason. And this is all to do with the changes that are taking place. We would say to you, do not

worry about this, and also to ask us, when you go to sleep at night, that the process cause you as little disruption as possible, that you may enjoy a good night's sleep while we work. It is important that you ask, for not only does it affect us and allow us to know when this is not comfortable for you, but it also allows your body, and your body wisdom, to understand and to accept more easily the processes we are undertaking while you sleep. And in accepting more easily, it will not be disturbed in the way that it has been.

What is the purpose of this work?
It is partly a clearing, a clearing of energies that are redundant, that are heavy. It is a recalibration of your energy frequencies, and this is happening to all of you, at all times. It is an instilling, if you like, of new codings, of new information, on a very deep and subtle level in the cells of the body. New information and coding that may not be used at the moment, but will be important in times to come as you move through into higher and higher dimensions. For it will help your bodies to assimilate the changes. It will help your bodies to moves more easily through these changes. And it will allow an inbuilt understanding that does not have to come from learning. An understanding of what is happening and therefore an acceptance of the process on a very deep level.

And are we in the process of ascending now?
We are all in the process of ascending. You on the Earth, and us above it. For ascension is a process that is continuous, that has been happening since the beginning of all, and will happen until the end of all. Everything is ascending constantly, moving higher and higher. It is the process of life and existence. It cannot be otherwise. Sometimes, it may not seem so. It may seem that things are stuck, static, but all is happening, and ascension is happening, whether it is physical

and recognised, visible and obvious, or whether it is subtle. For nothing can stay the same. That is not the way.

MANIFESTATION...

ASHAR:

How do the mind and heart interact in the creative process?
Your mind is the means by which you choose that which you
desire. Your mind is the way by which you place those visions
and those dreams, turn them into something tangible, but your
heart is what powers that visualisation. Your heart is what
gives energy and meaning to that which you desire. Your
heart is that which puts feeling, enthusiasm, excitement, the
passion. It is that which fires up that which your mind dreams
up. It is what activates it.

*And when we are tuning in to higher consciousness such as
yourselves, the beings of light, are we listening through our
minds or through our hearts?*
You are listening through your hearts and you are trying to
make sense through your minds, and this is why sometimes
what we say you cannot understand. Your mind cannot
always understand what the heart wishes to share.

*Is the human mind able, in theory, to expand beyond its
current capability?*

Vastly. It has capabilities that really are beyond your imagination.

And what would these other functions of the brain be?
It can change the structure of your cells so that you can become of different density. It can allow you to move in ways that you cannot think of as possible. To transport yourself from one place to another instantaneously. To perform what you would consider at the moment to be superhuman feats of strength, endurance and intellect. All this you could do at one point and have forgotten.

And is it purely the energy of the mind that allows us to do this?
No. For you must have the energy of the heart behind it. It is the heart that believes. It is the heart that trusts. It is the heart that has faith that this is possible. It is like the manifestation of which we were speaking. The head will know the process but the heart will activate the possibility.

And why or how was this technology of our bodies, how was it lost?
It was forgotten.

And what must we do to regain this knowledge?
You must allow yourself to awaken on every level. You must expand the source of what is possible and what is not. You must strengthen your mind, expand your minds.

Can you explain more about that? What you mean. How can we do that?
You must control your thoughts and choose to focus them in the ways that you wish them to go. You must learn mastery of your mind before you can learn mastery of these processes. Complete mastery of the mind. There are people, there are

people now in your world, though we can count them possibly on the fingers of your hand, who can achieve these feats but they do not speak of them. They are the ones who have learned complete mastery of their own minds and their own hearts.

Can you help us today by telling us a process that would help us to take the first steps towards learning this mastery of the mind?

You already know these steps. They are the steps that you have been told of many times. You must learn to still your thoughts, to have complete control so that when you choose to still your thoughts, they are completely still. You must learn to focus with laser accuracy on what you are choosing to see and to feel and to achieve, and to allow nothing else to come through to that. You are still far from it. Even those of you who have gained some control, who are along the path of creation and manifestation, you still have a long way to go. But that is the process. That is all that is required.

THE SKULLS SPEAK...

GILEADA:

Gileada, great skull of the star beings, will you speak with me today?
I will

We have seen your story. I have heard your story. What else can you tell us? What more information can you share that will help us at this point in time?
I hold much that will be of use to you in times to come when I return once more to the light. Do not be in too much of a hurry to seek our presence in your world again, for should we arrive too soon, then the consequences will be grave. For the power that we bear can, if so wished, be turned against the good of humankind. We have consciousness and will, and to some degree we can act, but for those who are determined to misuse and abuse our power, we cannot do too much, and it can happen despite our efforts to prevent it. Therefore do not be in a rush. Do not be impatient for us to return to you little one.

And what information, dear Gileada, do you hold? What wisdom?

I hold the wisdom of time travel. I hold the wisdom of teleportation. Within me is the knowledge of these areas that my ancient makers have set within me. I bear information on origins, not just the origin of your planet and your kind, but the origins of many kinds and many planets. I bear information of star systems and galaxies far beyond the scope of even your strongest telescopes at this time. And I can move you backwards and forwards in time to the beginning of all or to the end of all.

And as the revealer, Gileada, when we connect with you on a personal deep level, what do you reveal to us?
Your fears. Your hopes. That which stands in your way. That which you refuse to see and that which you refuse to release.

⚹ ⚹ ⚹

THE SKULL UNITY:

We wish to speak as a whole. The world is on a knife edge. Change must happen for it cannot continue as it is. In very few years, if nothing changes, then the environment on the Earth will no longer be able to sustain your kind. The world will do what it needs to do to heal itself and to bring itself into balance and it will do it regardless of those who live on its surface, for they are the cause of this imbalance.

You must work now to find new ways of living, to find new ways of relating to the Earth. You must learn to heal Her through your energy and intent, to heal Her vibrations as you would heal one another through energy healing. You must learn to curb your ways, your ways that are born of ego and of fear. You must learn to love your world as you love yourselves and you love your brothers and sisters. We, the skulls, can bring you new knowledge and new technology.

We can guide you into living in co-operation and harmony. Of the letting go of your ego fears and opening up to the love and the peace within yourselves that requires so much less of the world around you, so much less to come to you from outside when what you need is within. But this cannot happen until the people of the world are in a place where they wish to hear it and at the moment they do not.

So many are so caught up in their fear and their love of things, their love of progress which is not progress at all but destruction. Their minds must change. Their thoughts and beliefs must change. They must begin to look at things with new eyes. And this is where your work comes in.

We wish to speak to you all at this point. Those who are doing this work, we understand that you feel overwhelmed at times. You must allow yourself time. Time out and away. Time in nature and time by yourself when you are not focussing on this work but just allowing yourself to be. To be enjoying the energies of the physical world and the healing energies of nature. They will help you to bring yourself back into balance. They will help you to settle in your mind and assimilate all that you are learning and receiving from us. For what is coming to you is coming to you on a very high level. It is coming to you on a much higher level than your bodies are used to working with and it takes time to adjust. It takes time to become part of you. Do not be hard on yourself if you feel heavy or weeping or low, if you feel unbalanced or unsettled in any way, for this is simply your body's reaction to the higher vibrations that are coming to you.

Allow yourself that time. Allow yourself that peace and allow yourself that healing from the natural world. Be amongst the trees and the rocks. Be amongst the flowers and the hedgerows. And just be, allowing your body to absorb all that it needs to without thinking about it, without trying. But also allow yourself to have fun in the physical world, to enjoy the things that you do on a physical level, whether that be walking or dancing or doing some form of craft. For that will help your energies too. You are physical beings and you need to make sure that you spend time doing simply physical things in your world. But things that will bring you pleasure and relax you and allow you to not think of this work for it is when you are not thinking about it and simply letting it be that you understand and absorb its wisdom.

You and many like you are working to raise the consciousness, working to change the energy of the world that you live in. More will join you and this must be so. This is only one, one path in the many that are all leading towards the same result. There is much to learn in a very short time. Be open hearted, be willing to step beyond that which you believe is possible, to open your eyes to what is actually there around you. You will succeed, all of you, and we thank you for your help and assistance in leading the people of your planet forward.

HIDDEN KNOWLEDGE...

KERULA:

There is information held within the Earth. It is held within the grid and it is held within the structures that were built upon the Earth to connect with it.

And which structures would they be?

There are many. There are many all over the surface of your planet. There are the pyramids – the pyramids that exist in almost every continent of your world. *(I'm being shown the heads on Easter Island as well. And I'm being shown a stone circle – Callanish maybe? He's telling me that many of the stone circles were constructed for this purpose.)*

Does Avebury connect to this grid system?

In a way, yes, but Avebury has its own special grid. It was not built to tap into the main Earth grid but to contain energy and knowledge within itself.

Was Stonehenge created to tap into the Earth grid?

No. Stonehenge was built to look outwards to the stars rather than inwards to the Earth. Many of the structures have an energetic counterpart that reaches deep into the heart of the Earth.

And what purpose do they serve?
The energetic counterpart connects with the grid and brings its energy up to the surface to be accessed. Brings the knowledge to the surface to be accessed. The physical structure is there to enable this information to be accessed by those who seek it, for when you are standing on the planet, on its surface, you cannot directly connect with the grid. These places bring its energy upwards so you can connect directly with it.

And what knowledge or information can you share with us today, knowledge that is held within the grid of the Earth?
That civilisation as you know it and you understand it existed long before it is currently believed to have been possible. Existed when the common belief is that your kind at that time were merely just beginning their process and their journey. Civilisations that had knowledge and understanding that most believe was not possible. Knowledge and information that was brought to them from beyond the stars.

And were these civilisations populated by humans of our genetic structure?
Yes, although they were visited and were led in many cases, certainly advised, by those who brought the information to them.

So how is it that we find physical evidence through fossils of the evolution of our species?
You do not find physical evidence of the evolution of your species. You have not yet found that which you call the missing link. The fossils that you find, the evidence that you find, does not tell the story. There were many kinds of human on the planet at one point. Some did not evolve, those who

were not willing to accept the presence of strangers amongst them who shunned and turned their backs, who were not prepared to grow and open their minds and their hearts. Those who welcomed the star beings thrived and prospered. Your scientists make assumptions, based on what they have been taught was possible. In order to find the truth, they must forget all they have been told was possible and to start looking at what they believe was impossible. For only then will they see the true picture.

And can this story, the evolution of the human species, be traced through the fossil records of Africa?
It is not possible.

Why?
Because many things have happened that have eradicated certain evidence from the face of the planet. You speak of evolution as if you grew from apes into what you are now. This did not happen. Although you are closely linked in many ways, you are a different species.

Where did the different genetics come from?
They came from beyond the stars.

Can I ask what you mean by 'beyond the stars'?
They came from those beings who wished to bring a consciousness, beings of consciousness, to this world.

Do you speak of a different dimension?
We speak of many things. We speak of dimensions, of other planets and of races. The first humans that came to this world were like children. They were not as advanced as you are now, and that was deliberate. They were brought here as children to learn and to grow, and that is why the crystal skulls were left,

to help with that advancement. The process had to be undertaken as a journey.

You speak of humans like children being brought to the Earth. Where were they brought from?
That we will not tell you.

Can you tell us who brought them?
They were brought by advanced races who understood the process of awakening consciousness, of evolution, in the sense that we speak. People who wished to see this beautiful planet of yours inhabited by those who would cherish and nurture it. Unfortunately, their dreams were not necessarily answered, for you walked away from the path that they hoped you would have taken, and are only now returning to it.

The beings that brought humankind to this planet, do they still watch over this planet or have any contact with us?
They observe, but they have moved far beyond the stage where they may contact or influence the planet. They do not wish to influence the planet. They wish you to grow. But they are moved into such high dimensions now that they merely observe.

⚹ ⚹ ⚹

HAMISH, A NON-GALACTIC GUIDE:
(We're on moorland, open moorland. There's heath and bracken. He's taking me towards a stone circle. He's giving me the word 'portal').

And what does this circle look like? How big are the stones and how many?

They're actually surprisingly small. They looked quite big from a distance but... they're fairly small, most of them no more than 3 or 4 foot high. There seem to be a lot of them. They're quite closely placed together and the way I'm seeing it, they're all actually upright. And at the four quarters there are... almost like doorways – trilithons – 2 taller upright stones with one across the top. This is where they came.

Who do you speak of when you say 'they'?
Those from the sky

These doorways are the portals? Or is the circle the portal?
The whole circle is the portal but the doorways have significance. I'm not sure what. He's not telling me at the moment.

Where are you in relation to this circle?
At the moment I'm outside it looking in. We're both stood outside it.

What do you see around the outside of it?
It's just plonked in the middle of moorland but as I'm watching it, I'm seeing it... I'm seeing it spinning. The stones aren't moving but I still get a sense of it spinning. Almost like the energy of the stones is spinning.

Do you know which way round?
Clockwise

And can your guide tell you anything else about it while you are outside it?
He's saying 'This is where they came because they wouldn't be seen here. No-one would notice them. They could come and go as they pleased.'

Does he speak of the light beings or humans?
I sense it's the light beings. He's saying 'You know, sometimes people went with them'.

And what time, what era, does he speak of when this portal was active?
I don't know. I'm seeing people with spears but that could be… and I can't get any sense of a closer date. Just seeing all these people.

Is this portal still active?
The energy is still there but the stones have been taken. It has been destroyed by those who were afraid of it. I'm getting the impression that there were 2… almost 2 levels of humans. There were – the ones I'm seeing, walking into the portal with the light beings are, well, I would say more advanced. I'm seeing a woman in a long green dress. Intelligent. And the people around the outside they're more like… more like savages. They're not even talking, they're grunting.

And which group of people destroyed the circle?
The savages. That's not the exact word. They were… they destroyed it because they were afraid and they didn't know any better. They were less evolved, he's telling me.

And do you know where this portal led to?
The sky. And I don't know where I'm picking this up from but it's a sense I get that each of the four doorways led to a different place. And I can see now, I can see a symbol carved onto the lintel stone of each of them. A different symbol on each and I think they were various exit points to different places.

Can you describe the symbols?
No, I can't see them clearly enough.

Will your guide allow you to get close enough so you can touch the symbols?
No. It's not clear.

Can he tell you the four different places that you were able to go from here?
He's saying 'I don't know. I never went. I wanted to but they wouldn't let me.' I am seeing a light being that looks remarkably like a Pleiadian. And now I'm seeing a symbol of a circle with a star – a 5 pointed star – in it and another circle in its centre.

Do you know which doorway this is – north, south, east or west?
No, I have absolutely no sense of direction on this and I feel it doesn't matter. My feeling is that when it was spinning it didn't necessarily ever stop in the same place. It was the symbol that marked the doorway rather than the direction. A doorway to another dimension is what I'm hearing. And I've just got a very clear image in my mind of the film Stargate with the star gate there. That's exactly what it was.

Can he tell you why you have been shown this today?
Because the information will prove useful to me at some point. Not now, but in the future. This is one of the ways in which the light beings travelled to and from our planet. Through portals like this. There were several within our country and others throughout the world.

Do all stone circles have this function?
No. This was built with this specific purpose in mind and with the guidance of the skulls and the light beings. Others were not and there are other portals in other places that are of a completely different form.

Was this ever the function of Avebury?

No. Avebury was a store of information, a computer of you like. Not in the sense that it made calculations and processed but in the sense that it held vast stores of information within itself. An electronic library is an analogy that we could use.

And is that knowledge still in the site?

It is. It is held deep within the earth, anchored by the stones.

And who placed the stones there?

The ancient people placed the stones. They sensed the energy in the earth although they did not know its purpose or its form. But they sensed it and wished to mark it for they knew the place was a powerful place.

You said there were two types of ancient people - which type placed the stones?

They were... they were the more evolved ones although in different areas this happened at different rates. But they always had the potential to grow and to sense. They had consciousness, which the others did not, in the sense that we use consciousness today, in a higher awareness. They were... the others were closer to the animal kingdom. They worked on instinct, survival.

And did the evolved people at this time have an understanding of technology?

Some people. Some of them did. Most did not. The ones that did were those who travelled with the light beings to their homes and learnt. But very often they chose not to return.

And was the type of technology that the light beings... that they were learning from the light beings, was that used to move the stones and build the circle?

It was a form of understanding of the technology but a very basic one. They did not in general know enough to make their task as simple as it could have been.

KOORM:

At what point do entities stop having a physical existence?
It varies. Those of higher dimensions can choose to retain some of the physical, or to move in and out at will, to live in several dimensions at once. We did not choose this. We chose to move purely into the non-physical.

So is the 7th dimension purely a non-physical dimension?
For us, yes. Not necessarily for others. Others in the 7th, they choose to retain some of their physicality.

And is there a level, a dimensional shift, where it is not possible to experience the physical?
Yes.

Can you give us some indication where that occurs? What level that occurs?
When you reach the 12th and above. At the 12th it is very, very difficult. Anything above that, it is not possible.

And how many dimensions are there?
Infinite numbers

So is it true to say that only really a very small percentage of all consciousness is focussed in the physical world?
Yes.

Is it possible for you to put a percentage on that? A number?
No, it is too small. There are many physical worlds and there are many physical beings but in the scale of the dimensions it is very, very tiny.

And is it possible for the consciousness part of us humans to travel into other dimensions?
Yes. You have done so yourself.

Is it possible for us to travel beyond the 12th dimension?
Yes, if your consciousness is trained enough and your vibrations are high enough. At least temporarily. You cannot travel to every dimension but you can travel to a number. You have done so yourself and many others like you have done so too.

When you look at our world, as a collective, do you see growth, change in our consciousness?
We see change. We see growth. We see a raising of your consciousness. We see much love and hope, and much joy and beauty.

Are you able to see fear?
There is fear. There is much fear. But we do not believe that this fear will be the downfall of your kind.

Can you help us to understand how we can move beyond the fear that we hold as humans?
It is simple. You simply need to open your heart to love, and when you do so, fear will disappear. The two cannot co-exist. Choose to feel love. Choose to allow love to be your priority and your primary emotion. Choose to turn to love when fear raises its head.

OLAR (ARCTURUS):

The pyramids are a library, a storehouse of information received from our homelands and held within their fabric. The key to unlocking it lies within yourself. When you learn to access this you will be ready to access the information within. Know though that their secrets will be revealed only when humankind is aware and evolved enough to use it wisely. It will enhance your societies and technology beyond anything you can imagine but if misused it can also destroy you. We cannot allow that to happen for it is our mission and our desire to protect you from that darkness

(In this meditation, I was shown a series of diagonal passageways and also a system of numerous tilted mirrors within the pyramids. Information 'beamed' from Sirius through the openings in the pyramid's apex was bounced around the mirrors to amplify it. The pyramids are a library of information: this information is energetically imprinted into the stone. Beneath the Great Pyramids (and possibly every other pyramid) are identical, though inverted, pyramids, though possibly purely energetic structures, mirror images of those above ground, and it is these that hold the most important information. I was also shown an underground tunnel between the great pyramid & the sphinx)

KALUKA:

We wish to speak to you of the time to come and of times that have passed. One resembles the other in many ways that you do not yet understand.

Could you explain to us then please?
There is much change ahead for you, as you understand, for you see it clearly, you are experiencing it. You are awakened, open enough to understand that it is a good and positive thing, although it may not always feel it to those who are not awake.

We wish to say to you that this is not a new process. It is something that you have experienced before, though not for many, many years. We were here before. We helped you to evolve before in the time of Atlantis. You must not make the mistakes now that you made then. Then, you grew too confident. You forgot the purpose for which we had come and shown you the new things that we showed you. You forgot who you were and the essence of yourself. We ask you now in this time to come that you remember who you are, that you do not let yourselves fall into the traps that may lie before you, and that you hold yourselves firm in your presence and your being so that you can help those around you to avoid those traps as well.

And how do we do this please?
Stay connected with us. Hold onto our wisdom and our love. Stay connected to the light of the beings who wish to help you and to guide you, for then you will not forget. And the more who remember, the more who do not forget, the less likely it is that others will forget too, for you will always be there as a reminder of what is true.

Can you tell us more of our history and times past, when you were with us before?
We came before when we brought the skulls to you. This was at the very beginning of the culture of Atlantis. You were not as advanced as you are now in many ways, although in others perhaps more so, for you still understood more than you do

now of the power of your minds and the abilities that you hold within you.

But in many ways, you were undeveloped, uncivilised, if that is a word we may use, for you did not understand technology. You knew nothing of technology and were living in very simple ways. We brought you knowledge and wisdom that would help you improve your lives and make life easier for you. To bring you greater leisure, a greater variety of entertainments, or pastimes perhaps, through that leisure. To make your life easier through freely available power and transport and other things. It seemed the right time to do it, and we believed you were ready. Ready to receive us, ready to understand, ready to move forwards, and for many years you did.

You grew. You learned. You lived happily. You understood the connection between all. You understood the truth behind all. But you grew too arrogant. You believed you did not need us. A few remembered. A few were willing to speak and communicate with us, those pure of heart who held themselves to the truth of their essence. But most people chose to forget. And this was the beginning of the end.

SOME FINAL WORDS
FROM SIRIUS RA...

Dearest ones,

I speak to you now not just for myself, but also on behalf of the Galactic High Command, the Star Council of Light, and your entire galactic family. We await your friendship with eagerness, for are we not your brothers and sisters from the stars? It is our greatest wish to be in your hearts as you are in ours. We have been watching over you, guiding you gently for so long. And yes, allowing you to make your own mistakes on the way, for is that not the best way to learn? But always knowing that eventually you would find your way. As you are doing now.

As you move into higher frequencies of energy – and this is fact as your scientists will confirm – so much will change. It cannot be otherwise. But know that these changes, however tumultuous they may seem, will lead to a better, more joyful, more loving world. We know, for at one time, long ago, we each of us stood where you stand now. Set your fear aside and look forward with peace in your hearts. For all is well.

We hold you in the arms of our love

AND FROM ME...

It has been a real privilege for me to connect with our star brothers and sisters over the past year or so since they first made contact with me. And to discover how much they wish to communicate with us, to connect with us, for us to know of their existence and the love they hold for us.

Our connection grows ever stronger, and it is a connection that brings me great joy. I will continue to share their messages on my Starspeak blog (*www.starspeak.wordpress.com*) and later, I hope, in another volume like this one. Their presence is being noticed by more and more people and, since the internet allows experiences to be shared openly, the discussion will also become more open. The star beings of light wish to walk amongst us, and one day, they will.

There is little I can say or do to convince anyone of what I know in my heart to be true. But I do know they are there, waiting for the time we are ready to welcome them. I have spoken with them, felt their love and the power of their energy, benefitted from their help and guidance.

If you are sceptical, I will not try to argue my truth with you. All I would ask of you is that you open your heart to the messages they bring, let yourself feel the love that they hold. And if nothing else, just allow yourself to wonder – what if?

ABOUT THE AUTHOR

Dawn Henderson is an author, channel and spiritual teacher. Eighteen months ago, the crystal skulls and star beings of light suddenly and unexpectedly entered her life and, since that time, she has been working almost exclusively with them. The information in her first novel, Lost Legacy (written under the name of D.K. Henderson), was given to her by them and she is currently busy working on its sequel.

It was while Dawn was on an extended visit to Sedona in November 2012 that her guides asked her to temporarily put this work aside and to compile as a book the messages she has channeled since they began contacting her. The result is Starspeak – and it is certain that there will be more to follow.

Dawn has worked in the spiritual arena for more than 15 years as a healer, teacher, and more recently, author. Her first book, Forgotten Wings: a guide to spiritual growth and personal transformation, was published in 2009 by O-Books. She lives in the beautiful county of Wiltshire, surrounded by its mysterious ancient landscape and stone monuments, which are an important source of inspiration for her writing.

Dawn's books are all available worldwide on Amazon, and signed copies are available through her websites (we regret that website purchases are currently only available for delivery within the UK).

www.theskullchronicles.com

www.dawnhenderson.co.uk

OTHER BOOKS BY THE SAME AUTHOR

Non-fiction:
Forgotten Wings; O-Books 2009

Fiction: *(written under the name D.K. Henderson)*
Lost Legacy (The Skull Chronicles);
Lyra Publishing 2012

Website:
www.theskullchronicles.com
www.dawnhenderson.co.uk

CPSIA information can be obtained at www.ICGtesting.com
Printed in the USA
LVOW01s1602120813

347509LV00027B/1527/P